Best Wishes!

921b Elysian Fields Avenue

(RETURN TO SENDER)

by Catherine Moore

Catherine Moore
July 1, 2016

ISBN-13: 978-1517741297

ISBN-10: 1517741297

PUBLISHER'S NOTE

Names, characters, places, incidents, and other details have been changed, altered, or fictionalized to protect the privacy of those involved or to ensure the author's anonymity. Any resemblance to actual persons, living or dead, places of business, events, or locales is coincidental.

For more information on upcoming chapbooks, go to kystory.net.

921b Elysian Fields Avenue
(RETURN TO SENDER)

Dedication

For Joseph.

First of September 1987

Dear Daphne,

Water, is taught by thirst. Its cycle is the first lesson: tossed waters settled after a stormy night become the swill of street rills down drains and swoon across culverts to reharbor waves. The amphibians are unquenchable. We are all writhing sacks of the stuff. Even bones drink water. Our yearning never ceases for the divinity you drink from a tap. Frozen waterfalls, fountain springs, fog rising off Lake Pontchartrain—all three whisper amen. Last evening, I noticed the face of Jesus in a seepy levee and the Blessed Virgin weeping rain down a soft-lit window. In that overhead light, that moon moving our rivers without a fingerprint, that tells my brief parable.

Until our tide, Apollo

9/13

Babe,

It happened today. Again. Mist or smoke? I do not know. Just the morning hurling itself on my bed. I light up a cigarette. Push back into the insinuating blueness. No one likes us when we've slept badly. Last night the vaporous air around me took whatever made me human. I mourn my losses. I was a work in progress. Once.

When I consider, in all the clarity I can tune, what my life has become, it is deafening. I imagine the ordinary horrors of university hospital rounds, or endless gray TV dinners, or the long uninterrupted readings before sleep. How can you light the silent sky when I don't see you? Do you exist when I cannot touch you? A plausible reality suddenly hits me. I half rise from bed—human, convinced—you can see nothing, I envision everything. You wallow in silence, I am jazz. You are pale reflection, I am light. You are the possessed, I am the path. You must believe me.

Vern

Sept. 15, 1987

Daphne,

There are a thousand good reasons for being offended and angry (a complete siege of cranes! a murder of crows! a kit of carrier pigeons!). Notes from Vern need to stop. Yes, I regret the unfurled form of each letter, the curl on each serif word. I study myself in this text but I can't perceive it. I'm lost in the graphorrhea of my own hand.

You may wonder why my handwriting is so strange. For two reasons. The first, this Po'boy wrapper is too smooth and my pen glides right over it. The second is that I found, in the dormitory foyer, a delicious bottle of rum and I've already drunk half. The third reason is that there are only two reasons. I think the word *delicious* reminds me of you—excuse my moment of distraction.

You are my greatest distraction. Also the witching hour I sing, this liquor I drink, and the air I breathe. I never resist the alien sensations or the personalities that possess me. Vern and Apollo, they and you belong to the very way I exist. Am I what I seem to myself? To you? To

Vern or Apollo?

Do I really feel what I feel? I don't even know if it is *I* who feels. Maybe, my delicious, you know more than me, who I really ought to be?

Always, Paul

Fourteenth of October 1987

Dear Daphne,

Some days, I don't have the courage for blue at all and I remain congealed in gray. Blue is too close to waves and skies – devils on shoals – the vibrato, tremolo, falsetto, hoarse-voiced shouting – as the sun slow drags across the river's face. That is what I see looking up at the spirits looking down the delta.

And in this deepest down, I like the Mississippi best drenched with mud – unabashed in its brownish scowl, its puttied tail, like a dog left out in the sun too long. Aghast in the khaki of water, engulfed in the charcoal deep, there is not even ripple for a little blues. I listen for you, my angel.

Until song returns, Apollo

Oct. 17, 1987

Daphne,

You are hands, delicate and true, playing hide-and-seek with eyes of sky, the same hooded blue I knew in childhood. You are these lips of peaches, sometimes cranberry, that teach those yearned-for boyhood lessons. You are blackstrap legs, long as river beds, where I can nap in the mishap in between. At least in my dreams.

Always, Paul

Third of November 1987

Dear Daphne,

You do not have to be beautiful. You do not have to eclipse our harvest moons. Or shade a summer's day, out-luster rich sea gems, endear the outcast eye, draw phoenixes from ashes, free men with the sound of your fire, ornament a soprano's skill, awaken song from marble, plunge night back to dusk, drive the bee from clover. You do not have to be as unique as the leaves on grass. Even the grass howls of its common roots. Be the dirt, the soil, the loam. Be my fertile bed. My rest in the gaudy Spring. No, beauty is not for you, all the time.

Until something compares, Apollo

Nov. 4, 1987

Daphne,

All love letters are ridiculous. They wouldn't be love letters if they weren't. Equally, irrevocably, inevitably, ridiculous. That ode that compared your love to the shifts in tectonic plates: seismic, quaking, and shattering. The ode that compared my love to a volcano: fire, hiss, and hot lava. Man, if I could go back to when I wrote love letters without thinking: delete. Today my memory of those are how laughably preposterous (all more-than-three-syllable words, along with uncountable feelings, are also naturally, ridiculous).

Always, Paul

Tenth of November 1987

Dear Daphne,

Remember only this, every city has its moments of country quiet. Midday, when the fuss of yellow heat stagnates in the black green of trees. The villages inside cracks of pavement are the only tireless commerce. We lie in the haze of gray horizons and fictitious usefulness. Shade provides us a lazy animal way to watch wishes unfold. Our desire, in its splintering drifts, floats blithely by on the surface. I loiter for such a lovely day we don't even feel like dreaming.

Until then, Apollo

Dec. 24, 1987

Daphne,

I remember lying together on the park moss. At the top of the hill they built for sub-landia. We plotted our lives through the galaxy, pointing and winking like children, atop Monkey Hill. The clouds were fossil thin and the stars flickering through were flames for our clumsy first kiss. How close were the stars to Monkey Hill? On our tiny Everest we were Mars and Venus. Sun and moon. We were worshipper and goddess. We were mighty—above all the restrains of the deltaic plains. We were moments, and *joie*, and adolescents. The way we rolled down Monkey Hill. But the black tarp of sky cannot hold rain when it is time. And we lost our grasp in the deluge. And our paths in the downpour. This was the end of our evening's story—the way storms ravine down Monkey Hill.

Always, Paul

Jan. 2, 1988

Daphne,

Promise that you will make that midnight call. Stammered in fear. Staccato scared. Beg me the rescue. Promise you will invite me to your darkest moment.

I saved her this time. I broke through the door where she pounds like blood—push to shove, heave to scream. I threw light on the black of his intent. In that one swift move, in one quick dream, she became whole again. Without the specter of consent. Without apology for her biography. In the end it was a simple move, in dream.

We both know I failed to be that hero. It was a move I did not make, as courage came and went. This is now my torment. Promise you will call me in any event. I need the repentance.

Always, Paul

Third of January 1988

Dear Daphne,

You sail at dusk, although you didn't realize you are onboard until the sting of frigid spray nudges your cheeks. Then you sense the uneven sway of the tiny pirogue. It is an odd wake. The mist is freezing, locking lashes together, molding your sight. So you don't see the Tune Ship drifting past, your dangling hands nearly clear the wreckage, tranquil in all the cargo of life rafts, in a river of sorrow.

In slow thaw, you count the thirty-four corpses, elders who were left to drown in the river of Lethe. They now swim toward more fortunate isles. You lie, in limbo, watching, as they are swallowed in the waves of a million nobodies. Though you are unafraid under the keen gaze of an old man who just appears. Blue-eyes flash, a length of beard descends, by his haggard cheeks, a seaman. He is guiding this craft with a long pole.

As the sky brightens you reach. You reach, finally, to seize the punting pole and stop the propelling. Knowing that this is the moment, when the guardian of dreams ascends, and she will pull you back from the shoals. Stay with me.

Until a different day break, Apollo

1/11

Babe,

Of my many lessons: there is little room to write a love poem at the Camellia Grill. *Is she hot?* his whiskey-ed breath flames the side of my cheek. I came here trying for 1955, greasers, sharks and jets, Tulane men sporting bowties, ladies fretting about white gloves. I aimed to sit stool and counter, use linen napkins, unlined paper, and noir pen. The drunk turns back to his cohorts to boast. I've seen the dude crowd surfing at Shanahan's Pub.

A waiter pops the straws for a gaggle of hair-teased girls and artfully slides plastic out of paper into their colas. Next he shakes down sweet-n-low packets and dumps it synchronistic with coffee in my mug. Each movement is a volume, a rap session saying that I'm not doing the expected, to eat quick and leave. The cop slurping his free soup eyes me suspicious. Since there is little room for writing love poems at the Camellia Grill.

So is she? hot? My drunk counter-mate slurs again. Reaches for my journal. I push back with my shoulder. His sodden skeleton cascades off the seat, just nearly saved from a hard tile drop by my outstretched arm. He spins himself upright and hops in victory. Despite the promising blaze, this is not the room for writing love poems. At the bright Camellia Grill. *You boys want to dance, take it outside!*

Vern

Feb. 9, 1988

Daphne,

My boney nose and I confess we are largely bored. It is not the souring Midnight Jasmine or the shriveled Magnolias, I no longer smell the chicory in cafes on Market Street, or humid girls who live lights and music in barrooms bleached in soapy oils. Stale urine no longer stings. The salt on skin holds no ardor. I am heavy bored with the historical and the unspeakable, flushed in *Lem-O-Quat* disinfectant. Even the river spoils, and rum, smells like drag. I am rat, without whiskers, or discretion. Unashamed at a nibble, why must I taste every-thing? The invisible, the indiscriminate, all the indecent sniffs a city offers. I bide an air of contrition for this flatness. Perhaps Mass is in order this week?

Always, Paul

2/14

Babe,

Although I am writing to you, I hope only for an answer that will help me. I am seeking clarity but I am not thinking about you. I mean, after the last date snafu I've decided to let this situation be. Although I am writing to you, I wonder most about those girls at Sigma Nu—wanton, wild, like refugees. But I am not thinking about you. You in the tease, the taunt, the eschew. I the one who ends up as fallout debris. I'm through! Although I am writing to you only to say I've had this break-through and I hope that it will save me, and I am not thinking about you. I mean, I think the cure is a doctor's point of view, though I can't imagine what this could be. Don't answer. Although I am writing to you, I am never thinking about you.

Vern

Sixteenth of February 1988

Dear Daphne,

You ask, this ruminative, how is this bodily felt? Crammed with life dust gathered under nails or born large and looming in the hip's gape? Within arms stretched reaching to hold nothing, or inside chambers waiting to yield everything? Resting *sandhya* between each passing hale, rising in rings above a collar bone hollow, or hidden inside coils under the helix after floating in a tear duct pool? I don't know its dwelling but it is fluent, in the providential retreat of swallow, in the fortune of oscillating membranes.

Until that lucky meditation, Apollo

Feb. 18, 1988

Daphne,

I, too, am a man with obsessions. The photos enshrined. Pilgrim wanderings. Votive candles and holy water. There is a flood in me that cannot be contained. A river of thought, a current to the dendrites in my brain, even and true until it diverts. I am drown. I am dispirit. One lost self, inhabiting a self I cannot always find.

You don't need to understand. It is overwhelming. Especially as I watch the tides drift between us. I need to stop because I'm lost, and I've reached the end of this sheet, and this doesn't seem like it could be written by the hand of any other self, Vern, Apollo, but it was composed by me.

Always, Paul

Feb. 29, 1988

Daphne,

We lived our little drama. Whistled time away waiting for the tumble. A doomed watch just like the night the stars fell on Alabama. You kissed him by a river lit silver and white. I can't forget the tinsel, gleam of eyes, the hammering of pulse in ears, and his arms wound around you tight. In my imagination, at its flawless core, I see just you and me in the cascade of light, our own encircled heavens. Tonight, apparently the sky falls again. Although being an eve of ash and cloud, we won't see it coming.

Always, Paul

Babe,

The arrows don't line up. Their points are eroded by the roll of clumsy and thumbs. It's become a twist of no end, a roundabout plot that perturbs. A wring of pain. If I press, it will warp. I swelter in the agony of opening: with aspirin bottle tops, with painful conversations. The pop, the punk, I wish this entire mess uncapped instead of tightly wound. If only it was that simple. A quick slide. Like bodies diving off the *Riverboat Prez* during the *General Public* concert. So cool you're hot, hot, hot. Will there come a time when I understand, how much sweat I should invest in a life that won't last?

Vern

Ides of March 1988

Dear Daphne,

Blessed be all that is sacred. Sown together. Stitched as one. The doll with my X'ed eyes. I feel the green tranquility stabbed through its heart, of black giving relief to my mind, a pointed blue in my foot. As if to chant, drum, a hymn, this *Ve-Ve,* a wade through post-apocalyptic waters, and stop the drowning. Blessed be the resilient. The misnomered. The shalom in the wake of the storm.

Until the final barb, Apollo

Mar. 22, 1988

Daphne,

I retire to my room too often in the middle of the day. Is this a function of being a student, or having roommates? I don't know. I behave the same when the house is empty. The tin roofing seems less noisy back here in my haven, a sanctuary. Like the photo of you with that half-scowl. Such intensity with your eyes. I've placed it in the middle of the board. Your core, then spiraling out in emotion through the other twenty—the puzzled, saddened, candid, wicked and laughter.

Not all snapshots—there's broken shoelaces you threw away, a cocktail napkin from The Columns stained with your lipstick, an ash ring your coffee cup left on my notebook pages, the fallen hair clip rescued from a dance room floor (along with a jet curl entwined on it). And then the doubloon you tossed me at the Rex Parade.

It's the one thing I have that you gave freely. It will never cease to be mine. Despite the hunger I might feel, any urge within remains in the collect-ion. In gold, green, and purple, this lettered coin offering complimentary chicken at Popeye's holds more value than grub. I will stay hungry forever.

Always, Paul

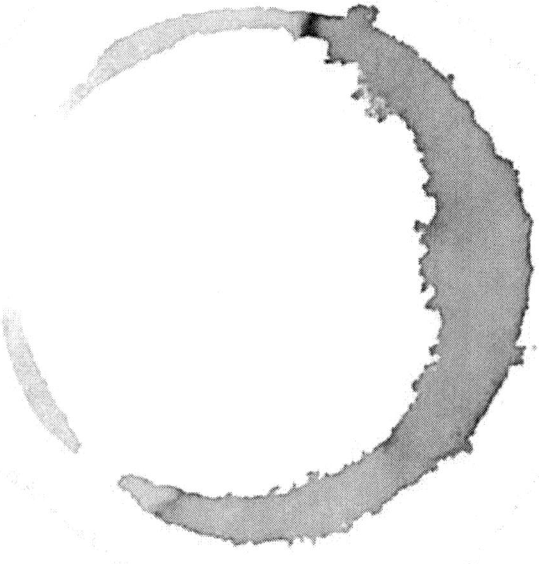

Apr. 1, 1988

Daphne,

We dissected a brain today. To find out why it stopped working. Inside dark spots, an emptiness where it climbed inside to die. To study of void of cells, like once bright stars faded to black holes. An eternal winter space in the meninges universe. Did it freeze the kissing urge first? Then loves' name? Do you know it all starts with one cell? Just one *nada*, one *no!* One steps out of sequence. Quits the dance. Hovers on the sideline to do, nothing.

After the lab, I saw a wedding rehearsal party dancing down the steps of the campus church. Watched the sexy bride dressed in red high heel shoes, her updo pin-curled like Betty Boop. *Oooh, what a lovely tether,* she said playfully tugging on her groom's tie. I thought she might have ended with a *boop-boop-de-doop*! But that's probably the formaldehyde talking.

Always, Paul

Second of April 1988

Dear Daphne,

Darkness is simply part of the whole. It makes the other bright and beckoning like fiolet, that eerie burning gently floating us towards brackish waters. We garnish beryls and rosemary amulets then swim into the moon-less bayou. Pray it cradles us above the waterline.

Until a light for this starless swamp,
Apollo

Apr. 28, 1988

Daphne,

I almost thought I saw you dance with rutabagas on the streetcar. Well, maybe eggplant not rutabagas. Either way it was good to see you happy. Well, perhaps not happy as much as delirious. Or debauched. An intoxicating change from a mundane ride—reeling with a cast of costumed dancers. The sight of furtive fruit became transcendental. I might have joined you. We might have laughed all night, inebriate of air, it could have been intimate. I may owe you an apology. Here, it is offered now while still ripe.

Always, Paul

First of May 1988

Dear Daphne,

I admire the gnarled loveliness of a found Cotton Rose, while wrapping this note around its shrub-cut stem. I chose this for its lack of artifice—unpruned, thrust in imperfection. The bloom appears as a basket of grubby ruffled hands that beg for skylight, with pleas to extend its one-day life. But, nothing will save the morning white from withering to blood red before death. This certainty begins on the edges where affections wait, desiccates to rust, and falls in a brittled crash like porcelain.

Until the last shade, Apollo

May 9, 1988

Daphne,

This is just to say, by now you have discovered my theft. My crime by comparison to yours is pale. A stolen photo for a stolen heart, sweetest thief, you are cruel to your most faithful follower. Everyone is at fault. Even I in committing this crime. It called for my touch. The photoed one I've been looking at so long, like the image of a young Elizabeth Taylor kissing sky. Full in lips and eyes and smiles. Bright, delicate, fallen.

But, a Taylor it seems of the lesser gods (see, both my love and hate in such civil wars.) I am so torn. My cloudy thoughts eclipse both the moon and sun. If I wanted you to feel me, I'd include all the lyrics to the song I'm singing. For now: "If only I'd thought of the right words..."

I left our spiced lotions, slow-burn candles, the Prince albums, piled stoop-side. For you, probably a St. Vincent DePaul donation. I'll forgive you for the losses, so callus and so cold.

Always, Paul

5/12

Babe,

Sometimes you don't want to hear me. Even in deafening night I am foot whisper, am early dew—I disturb you. You will sense me in the squish of damp carpet underfoot, your wet and wrinkled skin. In the deepest side of you, burrowed in waking and in sleep, you must always hear my scratch. In the scurry past water rising, in late chills and shivers, in this, I am your master, *myocastor coypus*, beast of your dreams. Inevitably, you will follow the canals in my mind beyond the floating debris of truth and once there, it may rescue you.

Vern

Thirtieth of May 1988

Dear Daphne,

I left at 6 a.m. without farewell. Apologies. The blotches on this page are made from rain. Deluge sprayed through a window crack all the way from Loyola Avenue to Baton Rouge. Not an ounce of sun today. Nothing will cure. How gray precipitations parch my spirit. How the drone of a motor is Ferris wheeling to my thoughts.

I have dry lips, from whispering to you, and my head burns, wanting to sing with excessive expression. Ah, to be able to express myself wholly the way a motor coach does. Rend myself totally, exhaust myself, make myself permeable to the perfume of gasoline and heat and oil. Surrender my hand to a near-silence in the monotony of transmission belts.

I don't know how far I will go this time. Life is as mysterious as this Greyhound station continually crossed by people. A lobby accessible to any and every thought, real, impossibly real, certain, unknowingly certain. I wait with destiny driving the coach of everything down the road of nothing. Or maybe I'll

stay in the painful light of fluorescent
lamps. I have a fever and I write.

Until the empty coach departs, Apollo

Jun. 1, 1988

Daphne,

Go tell everyone. Don't you remember, the blue-tongued devils await your words. When was the last time you thought of me? Never mind, I can't keep you anymore. Let it go, let it be, let it burn.

Go set fire to the levees. See the blur between the night city and a black heart. Don't let the miracle of the fall pass you by. I'll be the only one to know, what made you let go.

Go burn. I'll not ask you now. Now while my letters go unanswered and yours go unconsumed. I let you go. Until you turn up again, in a dream of blue flames.

Go find him. Glow in the love you want, I won't remain. Go. I'll try to forget the scorch of hunger all the time. Go let the starvation begin.

Always, Paul

August 1988

Paul,

I enclose your letters—water cured, crisp as cockle onion skin, ragged flapped, yet unopened. Also your lovelorn artifacts, some rescued from the slash and burn before Daphne left.

Dude, the lot of it—all the photos along with the stuff ya'll hauled like sewer rats out of the Vieux Carré: knickknacks from the Napoleon House, Pat O' stemware, cocktail stirrers from the Olde Absinthe, and every conceivable matchbook cover. I imagine you can light the world on fire with what is left behind. If I hear from Daphne, it might be the end of days, and I'll send up a flare.

Charlene

p.s. keeping the Madame Flame Love Voodoo condoms—priceless!

About the Author

Catherine Moore's writing has appeared in *Tahoma Literary Review, Southeast Review, Silver Birch Press, Southampton Review*, and in anthologies most recently by *Pankhearst Press*. Her work garnered the 2014 Gearhart Poetry Prize and has been selected for inclusion in *The Best Small Fictions of 2015*. Her chapbook *Story* is available with Finishing Line Press. Catherine has a M.F.A. from the University of Tampa. Her twitter handle is @CatPoetic.

Acknowledgements

After attending translator-scholar Richard Zenith's lecture on Fernando Pessoa while at DISQUIET: International Literary Program in Portugal, I was fascinated by Pessoa's use of heteronyms (variety of personas/pen names) in his private love letters. That fascination served as inspiration for this collection.

I gratefully acknowledge my first readers Alfred Booth and Suzanne Richter who both fell obsessively for my lovelorn protagonist(s); though each with a love for a different heteronym.

50400410R00024

Made in the USA
Charleston, SC
19 December 2015